Ed Sheeran
FOR UKULELE

Cover photo by Christopher Polk/Getty Images for Wonderwall

ISBN 978-1-4950-1739-1

HAL•LEONARD® CORPORATION
7777 W. BLUEMOUND RD. P.O. BOX 13819 MILWAUKEE, WI 53213

Visit Hal Leonard Online at
www.halleonard.com

The A Team

Words and Music by Ed Sheeran

team, stuck in her day - dream. Been this way ___ since

eight - een, ___ but late - ly ___ her face seems ___ slow - ly sink - ing, wast -

- ing, crum - bl - ing ___ like pas - tries. And they ___ scream: The worst ___

___ things in ___ life come free to us, ___ { (1., 2.) 'cause we're
{ (D.S.) and we're

Chorus

just un - der the up - per hand ___ and go mad for a cou - ple grams. ___
all un - der the up - per hand ___ and go mad for a cou - ple grams. ___

And she don't wan - na go ___ out - side ___ to - night. ___ And in a
And we don't wan - na go ___ out - side ___ to - night. ___ And in a

To Coda

pipe she flies to the Moth - er - land, __ or sells love to an - oth - er man. __

pipe we fly to the Moth - er - land, __ or sell love to an - oth - er man. __

It's too cold _____ out - side _____ for an - gels __ to fly. __

1.

__ An - gels __ to fly. _____

2.

Bridge

_____ An an - gel __ will die __

cov - ered in ___ white, closed eye ___ and

hop - in' for a bet - ter life ___ this ___ time. We'll fade out to -

- night straight down the line. (Ooh. _____

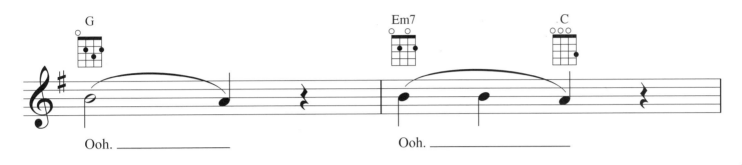

Ooh. _____ Ooh. _____

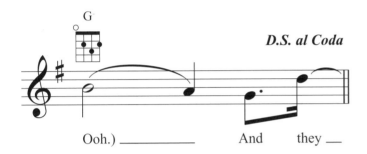

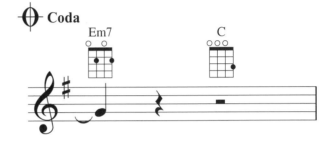

D.S. al Coda

Ooh.) _____ And they ___ _____

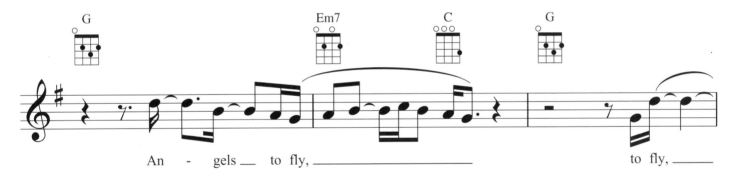

An - gels ___ to fly, _____ to fly, _____

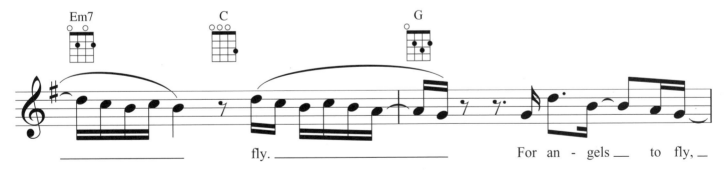

_____ fly. _____ For an - gels ___ to fly, ___

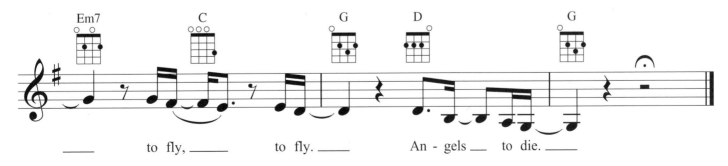

___ to fly, _____ to fly. ____ An - gels ___ to die. _____

All of the Stars

from the Motion Picture Soundtrack THE FAULT IN OUR STARS
Words and Music by Ed Sheeran and John McDaid

First note

Verse
Moderate Ballad

1. It's just an-oth-er night and I'm star-ing at the moon. ___
2. I can hear your heart on the ra-di-o ___ beat. ___

I saw a shoot-ing star ___ and thought of you.
They're play-ing "Chas-ing Cars" ___ and I thought of us,

I sang a lull-a-by by the wa-ter-side and knew ___
back ___ to the time you were ly-ing next to me. ___

if you were here, ___ I'd sing to you.
I looked a-cross ___ and fell in love.

You're on the oth-er side ___ as the sky-line splits in two, ___
So, I took your hand ___ back through lamp-lit streets and knew ___

C

____ miles a - way ___ from see - ing you.
____ ev - 'ry - thing ___ led back to you.

G   Gsus4

F   C

But I can see the stars   from A - mer - i - ca. ___
So, can you see the stars   o - ver Am - ster - dam,

Am   G   F

C   G

I won - der: do ___ you see them, too?
hear the song our heart ___ is beat - ing to?

So o - pen your

Chorus

C   G

eyes and ___ see ___   the way our ho - ri - zons ___ meet. __

Am

And all of the lights will ___ lead ___   in - to the

F   C

night with ___ me. ___   And I know these ___ scars will ___ bleed, __

but both of our hearts be - lieve ____ all of these __

____ stars will __ guide ____ us __ home.

Outro

____ us __ home. And oh, _____ and oh, __

_____ and oh. _____

I can see the stars from A - mer - i - ca. __

Bloodstream

Words and Music by Ed Sheeran, Amir Izadkhah, Kesi Dryden, Piers Aggett, John McDaid and Gary Lightbody

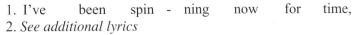

- ly ___ now. If you ___ loved ___ me, ___ how'd you nev - er learn? _

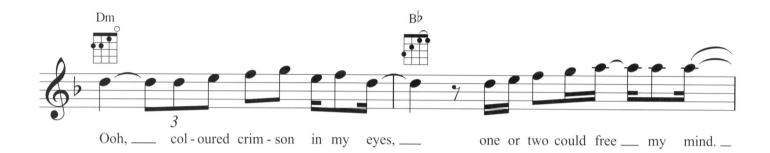

Ooh, ___ col - oured crim - son in my eyes, ___ one or two could free ___ my mind. _

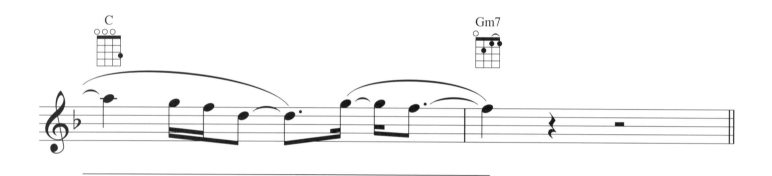

Chorus

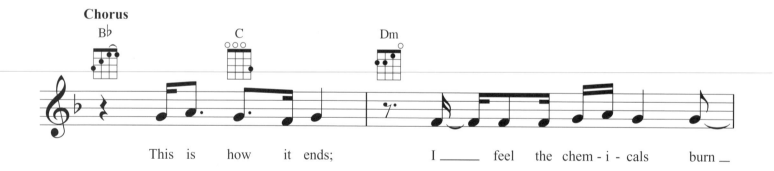

This is how it ends; I ___ feel the chem - i - cals burn _

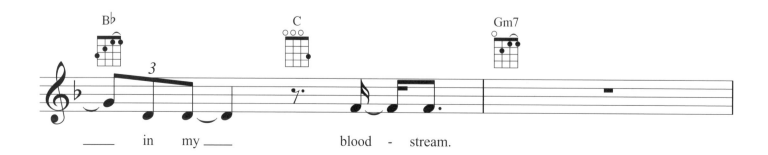

___ in my ___ blood - stream.

Fad - ing   out ___   a - gain,   I ___ feel   the   chem - i - cals   burn ___

___   in   my ___   blood - stream.   So,   tell   me   when   it   kicks   in.

Let chord ring.

Interlude

Mm, _____   mm, _____

___   Mm. _____   Well,   tell   me   when   it   kicks   in.

Mm, _____   mm, _____

1.

mm.

Bridge

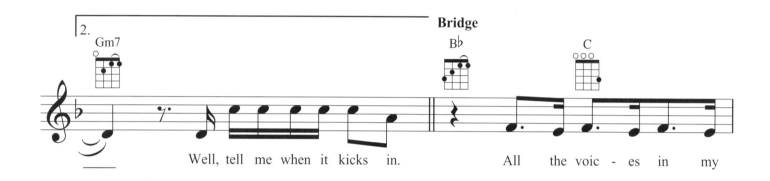

2.

mm.

Well, tell me when it kicks in. All the voic - es in my

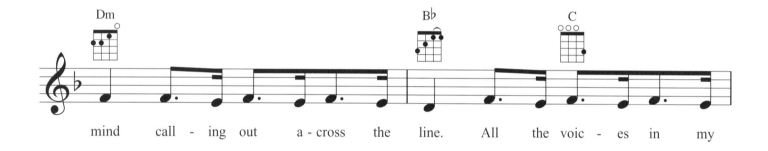

mind call - ing out a - cross the line. All the voic - es in my

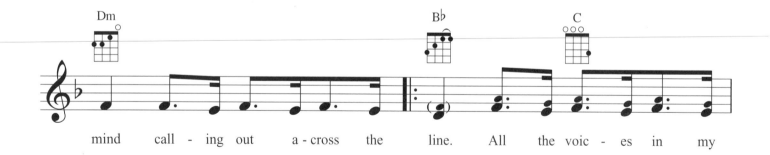

mind call - ing out a - cross the line. All the voic - es in my

mind call - ing out a - cross the line. All the voic - es in my

Additional Lyrics

2. I've been looking for a lover;
   Thought I'd find her in a bottle.
   God, make me another one.
   I'll be feeling this tomorrow.
   Lord, forgive me for the things I've done.
   I was never meant to hurt no one.
   I saw scars upon a brokenhearted lover.

Drunk

Words and Music by Ed Sheeran and Jake Gosling

First note

Verse
Moderately

1. I wan - na be drunk when I wake up
2. *See additional lyrics*

on the right __ side of the wrong __ bed, and nev - er an ex - cuse I made up.

Tell __ you the truth, I hate what did - n't kill me; it

nev - er made __ me strong - er at all. __

Love will scar your make - up. Lip sticks to me, __ so now I may - be lean

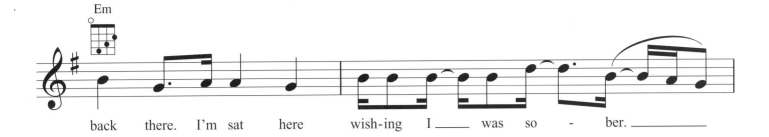

back there. I'm sat here wish-ing I _____ was so - ber. _____

I know I'll nev - er hold _____ you like I used _____ to.

Pre-Chorus

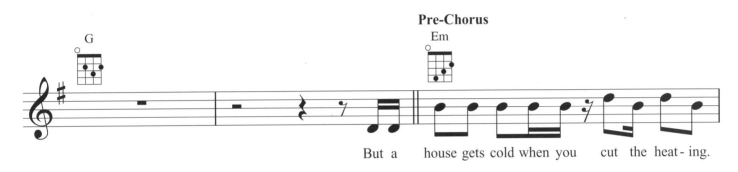

But a house gets cold when you cut the heat - ing.

With - out you _____ to hold, I'll be freez - ing. Can't re - ly on my heart to beat - in',

'cause you take parts of it ev - 'ry eve - ning. Take words out of my mouth just from breath - ing,

re - place with phras - es like _____ "When you leav - ing me?" Should I? Should I?

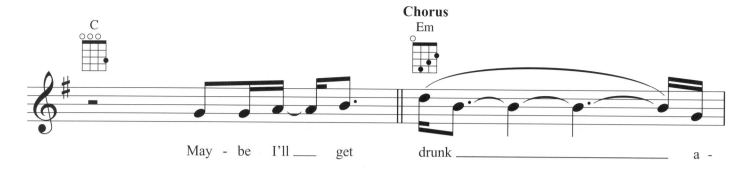

May - be I'll ___ get drunk _____ a -

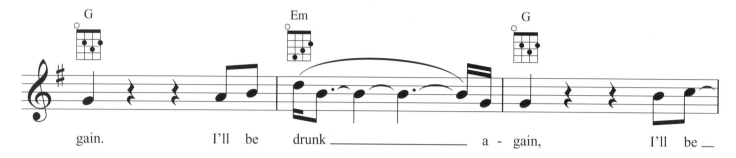

gain. I'll be drunk _____ a - gain, I'll be ___

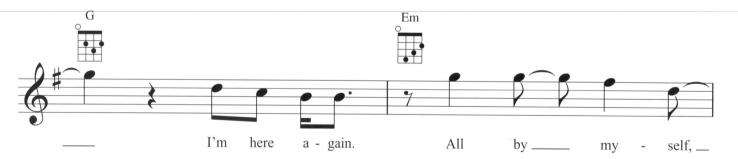

___ drunk _____ a - gain to feel a lit - tle

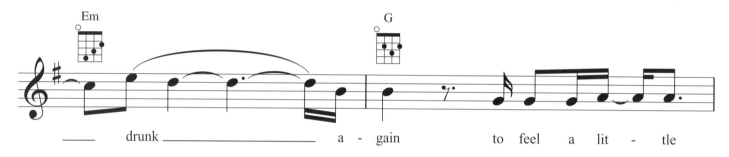

love. _____ All by ___ my - self, ___

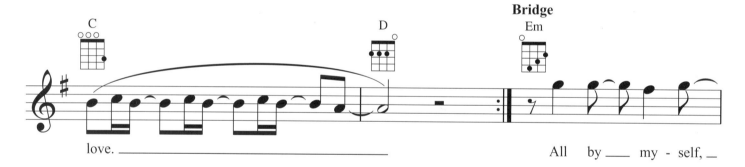

___ I'm here a - gain. All by ___ my - self, ___

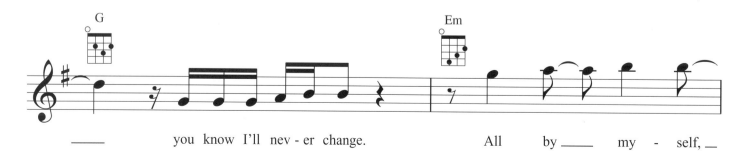

___ you know I'll nev - er change. All by ___ my - self, ___

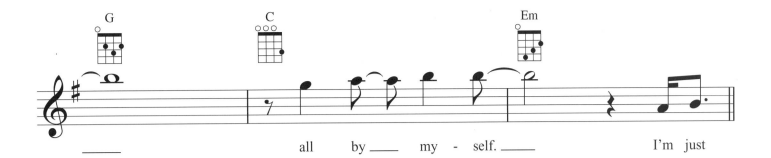

all   by ___ my - self. ___   I'm just

Outro-Chorus

drunk _____ a - gain.   I'll be drunk _____ a -

gain,   I'll be ___ drunk _____ a - gain   to feel a lit - tle

love. _____

Additional Lyrics

2. I wanna hold your heart in both hands,
   Not watch it fizzle at the bottom of a Coke can.
   And I got no plans for the weekend,
   So should we speak then, keep it between friends?
   Though I know you'll never love me like you used to.
   There may be other people like us
   Who see the flicker of the Clipper when they light up.
   Flames just create us, but burns don't heal like before,
   And you don't hold me anymore.

Pre-Chorus: On cold days, cold plays out like the band's name.
   I know I can't heal things with a handshake.
   You know I can't change, as I began saying.
   You cut me wipe open like landscape.
   Open bottles of beer, but never champagne,
   To applaud you with the sound that my hands make.
   Should I? Should I?

Give Me Love

Words and Music by Ed Sheeran, Chris Leonard and Jake Gosling

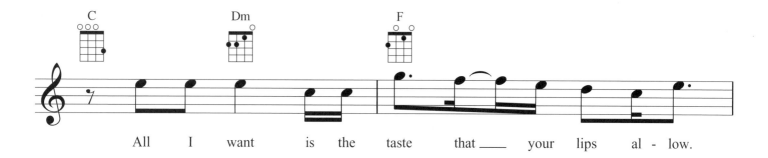

All I want is the taste that ___ your lips al - low.

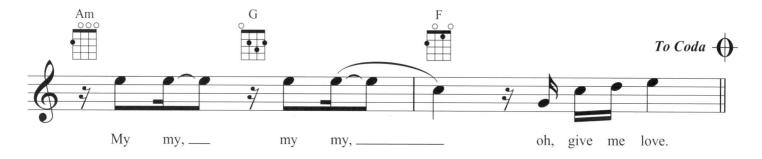

To Coda

My my, ___ my my, ___ oh, give me love.

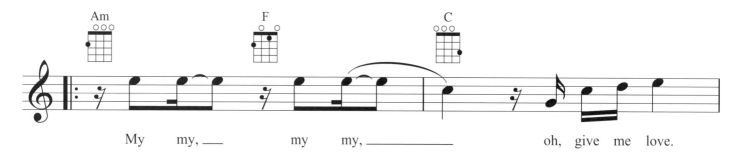

My my, ___ my my, ___ oh, give me love.

1.

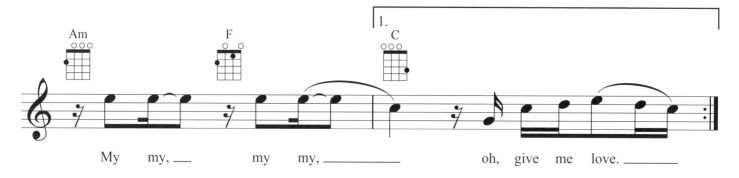

My my, ___ my my, ___ oh, give me love. ___

2.

Verse

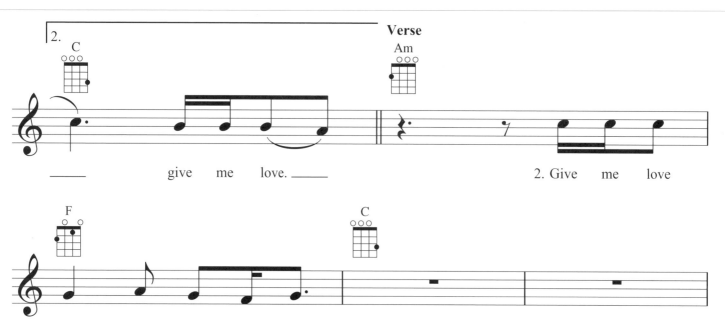

___ give me love. ___   2. Give me love

like nev - er be - fore.

D.S. al Coda

Coda
Chorus

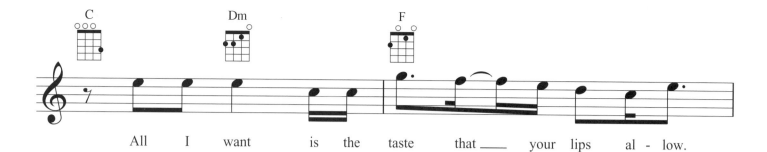

All I want is the taste that ___ your lips al - low.

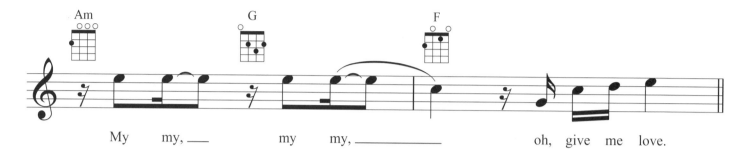

My my, ___ my my, _____ oh, give me love.

My my, ___ my my, _____ oh, give me love. My my, ___ my my, ___

1.
___ oh, give me love. _____

2.
___ give me love. ___

Interlude

Play 3 times

(M - my - my - a, m - my - my - a, m - my - my - a, gim - me love, lov - er.)

Play 3 times

M - my - my - a, m - my - my - a, m - my - my - a, gim - me love, lov - er.

I See Fire

from THE HOBBIT: THE DESOLATION OF SMAUG

Words and Music by Ed Sheeran

Oh, mist-y eye of the moun-tain be-low, keep care-ful watch of my broth-ers' souls. And should the sky __ be filled with fire __ and smoke, __ __ keep watch-ing o-ver Dur - in's sons.

1. If this is to end __ in fire, __ then we should

(2., 3.) *See additional lyrics*

all burn to-geth-er, watch the flames climb high into the night.

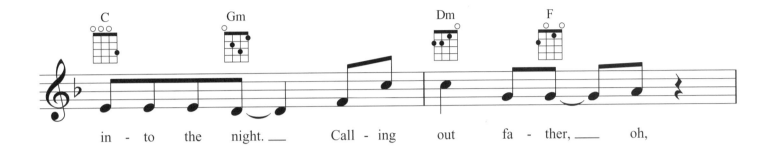

in - to the night. Call -ing out fa - ther, oh,

stand by and we will watch the flames burn au - burn on the

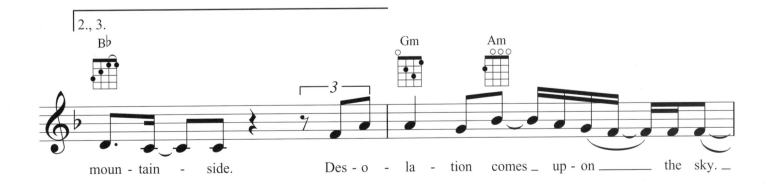

1.
moun - tain - side. 2. And if we should

2., 3.
moun - tain - side. Des - o - la - tion comes up - on the sky.

Outro

Additional Lyrics

2. And if we should die tonight, we should all die together,
   Raise a glass of wine for the last time.
   Calling out father, oh, prepare as we will
   Watch the flames burn auburn on the mountainside.
   Desolation comes upon the sky.

3. Oh, should my people fall, then surely I'll do the same.
   Confined in mountain halls, we got too close to the flame.
   Calling out father, oh, hold fast and we will
   Watch the flames burn auburn on the mountainside.
   Desolation comes upon the sky.

Don't

**Words and Music by Ed Sheeran, Dawn Robinson, Ben Levin,
Raphael Saadiq, Ali Jones-Muhammad and Conesha Owens**

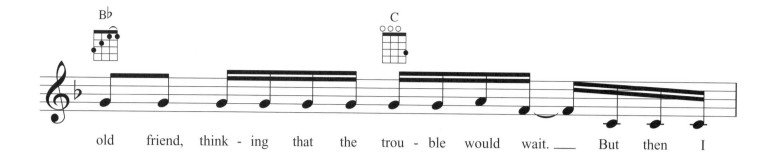

old friend, think - ing that the trou - ble would wait. ___ But then I

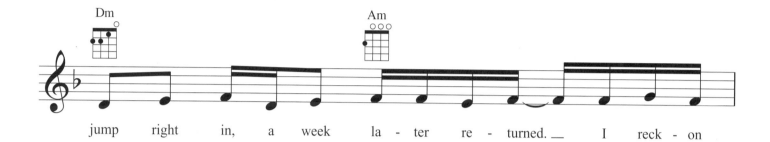

jump right in, a week la - ter re - turned. ___ I reck - on

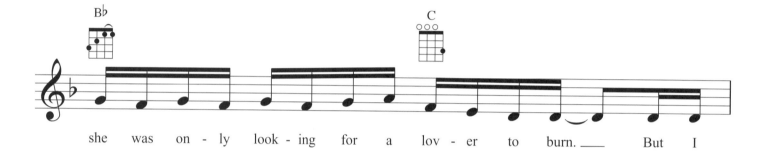

she was on - ly look - ing for a lov - er to burn. ___ But I

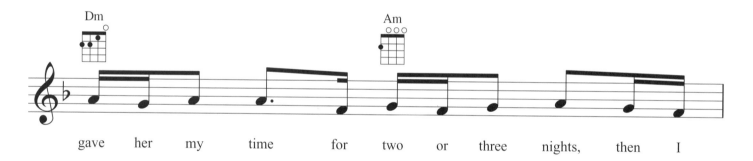

gave her my time for two or three nights, then I

put it on pause un - til the mo - ment was right. ___ I went a -

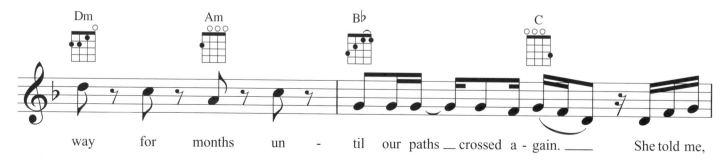

way for months un - til our paths ___ crossed a - gain. ___ She told me,

"I was nev - er look - ing for a friend. May - be you can

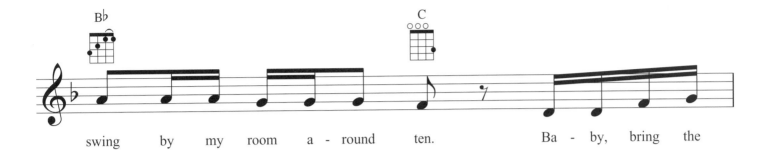

swing by my room a - round ten. Ba - by, bring the

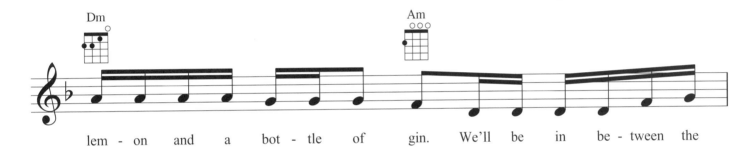

lem - on and a bot - tle of gin. We'll be in be - tween the

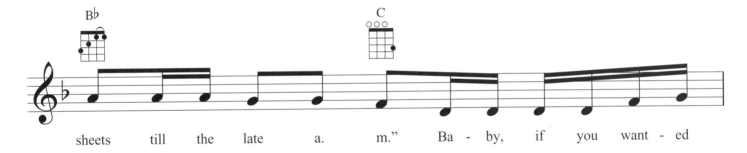

sheets till the late a. m." Ba - by, if you want - ed

me, then you should-'ve just said. She's sing-ing: Ah, la 'n la _____ la.
Don't **** with my

Chorus

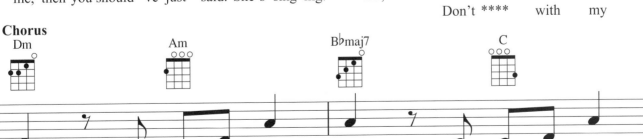

love. That heart is so cold all o - ver my

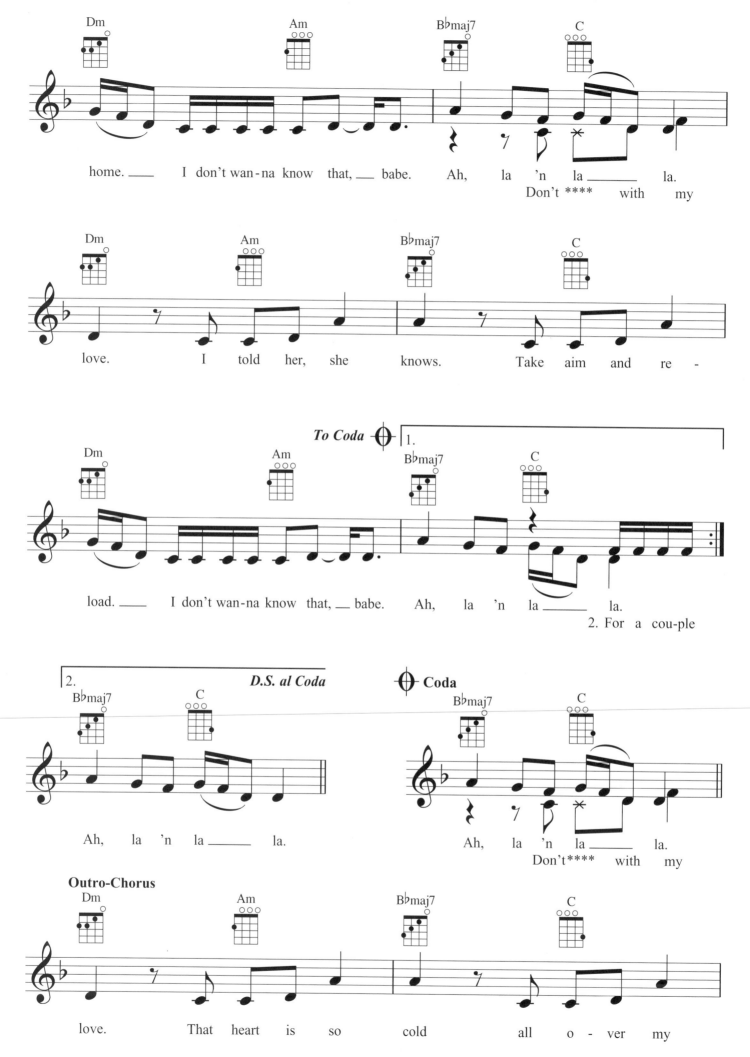

home. ___ I don't wan-na know that, ___ babe. Ah, la 'n la _____ la.
Don't **** with my

love. I told her, she knows. Take aim and re -

load. ___ I don't wan-na know that, ___ babe. Ah, la 'n la _____ la.

Additional Lyrics

2. For a couple weeks I only wanna see her.
   We drink away the days with a take-away pizza.
   Before, a text message was the only way to reach her.
   Now she's staying at my place and loves the way I treat her.
   Singing out Aretha all over the track like a feature,
   And never wants to sleep; I guess that I don't want to, either.
   But me and her, we make money the same way:
   Four cities, two planes the same day.
   And those shows have never been what it's about,
   But maybe we'll go together and just figure it out.
   I'd rather put on a film with you and sit on the couch,
   But we should get on a plane or we'll be missing it now.
   Wish I'd have written it down, the way things played out
   When she was kissing him, how I was confused about.
   Now she should figure it out while I'm sat here singing:

3. *(Knock knock knock)* on my hotel door.
   I don't even know if she knows what for.
   She was crying on my shoulder; I already told ya:
   Trust and respect is what we do this for.
   I never intended to be next,
   But you didn't need to take him to bed, that's all.
   And I never saw him as a threat,
   Until you disappeared with him to have sex, of course.
   It's not like we were both on tour.
   We were staying on the same **** hotel floor.
   And I wasn't looking for a promise or commitment,
   But it was never just fun and I thought you were different.
   This is not the way you realize what you wanted.
   It's a bit too much, too late, if I'm honest.
   And all this time, God knows, I'm singing:

I'm a Mess

Words and Music by Ed Sheeran

in - side my eyes. _____ It burns so

bright; _____ I wan - na feel your ___ love.

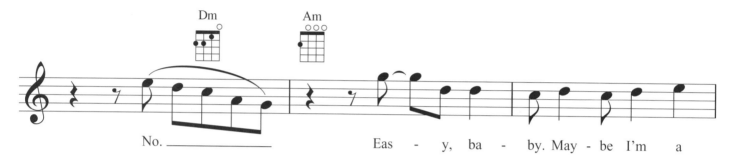

No. _____ Eas - y, ba - by. May - be I'm a

liar, _____ but for to - night, _____ I

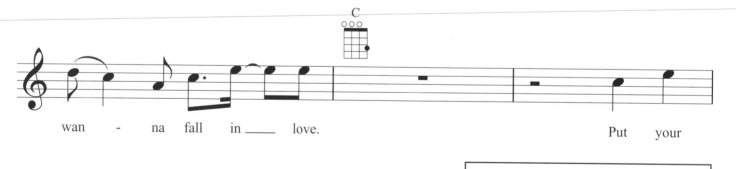

wan - na fall in ___ love. Put your

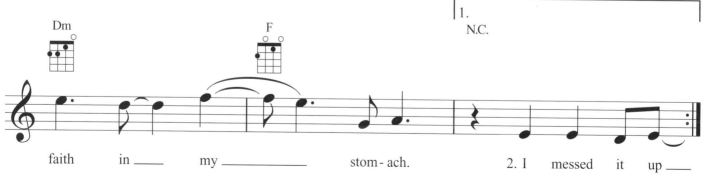

faith in ___ my _____ stom - ach.   2. I messed it up ___

1.
N.C.

Kiss Me

Words and Music by Ed Sheeran, Julie Frost, Justin Franks and Ernest Wilson

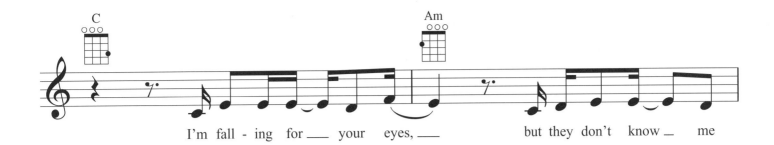

I'm fall - ing for ___ your eyes, ___ but they don't know ___ me

yet. And with a feel - ing I'll ___ for - get, I'm in love now.

Chorus

Kiss me ___ like you wan - na be loved, you wan - na be

loved, you wan - na be ___ loved.

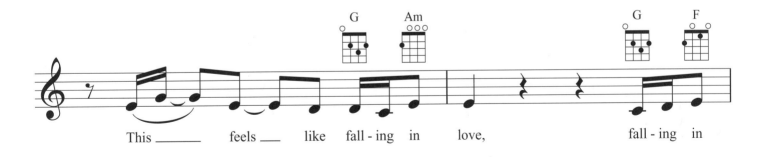

This ___ feels ___ like fall - ing in love, fall - ing in

To Coda ⊕

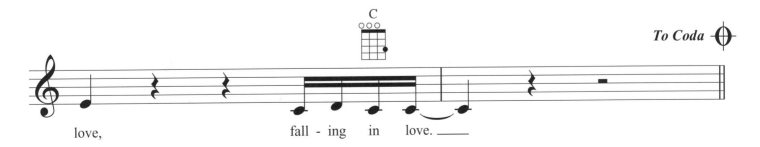

love, fall - ing in love. ___

Verse

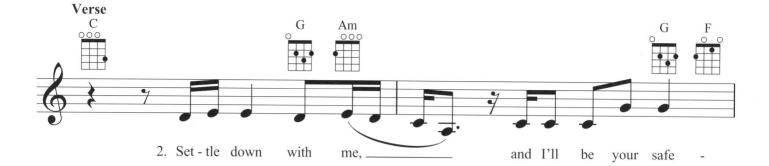

2. Set - tle down with me, _____ and I'll be your safe -

ty, and you'll be my la - dy.

I _____ was made _____ to keep _____ your bod - y warm, _____ but I'm

D.S. al Coda

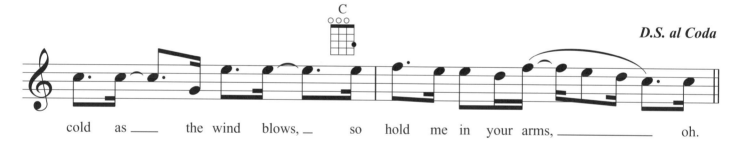

cold as _____ the wind blows, _____ so hold me in your arms, _____ oh.

Coda

Bridge

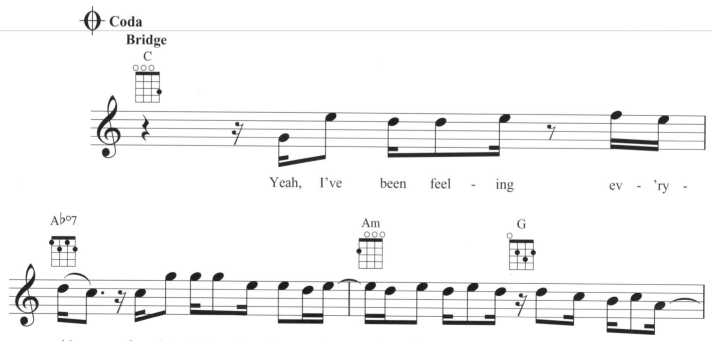

Yeah, I've been feel - ing ev - 'ry -

thing _____ from hate to love, from love to lust, _____ from lust to truth. I guess that's how I know _____

Outro-Chorus

41

Photograph

Words and Music by Ed Sheeran and John McDaid

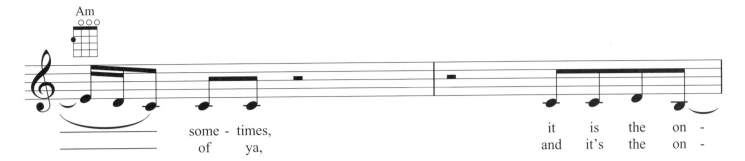

some - times,
of ya,

- ly thing ___ that makes ___ us feel a - live. ___
- ly thing ___ we take with ___ us when we die. ___

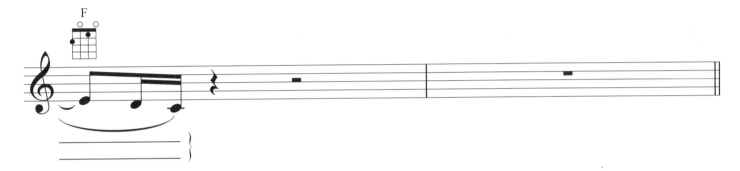

Pre-Chorus

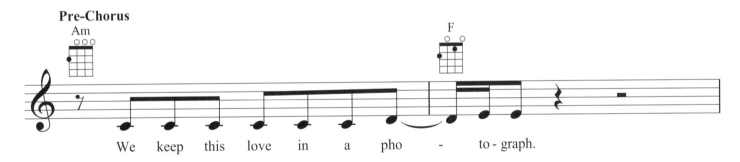

We keep this love in a pho - to - graph.

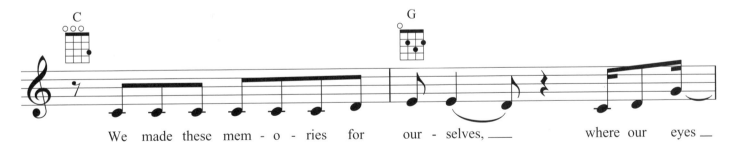

We made these mem - o - ries for our - selves, ___ where our eyes ___

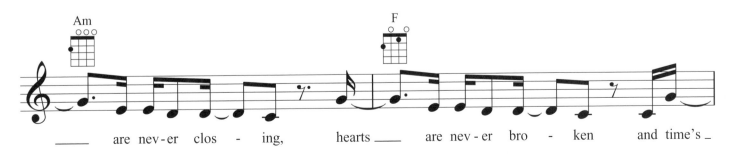

___ are nev - er clos - ing, hearts ___ are nev - er bro - ken and time's ___

_____ for - ev - er fro - zen still. So you can

𝄋 Chorus

keep me in - side the pock - et of your
(D.S.) fit me in - side the neck - lace you got _____ when you were

ripped jeans, hold - ing me clos - er till our
six - teen, next to your heart - beat where I

eyes meet, and you won't ev - er be a -
should be. Keep it deep _____ with - in your

1.

lone. Wait for me to come home.

N.C.

2. Lov - ing can heal, ___

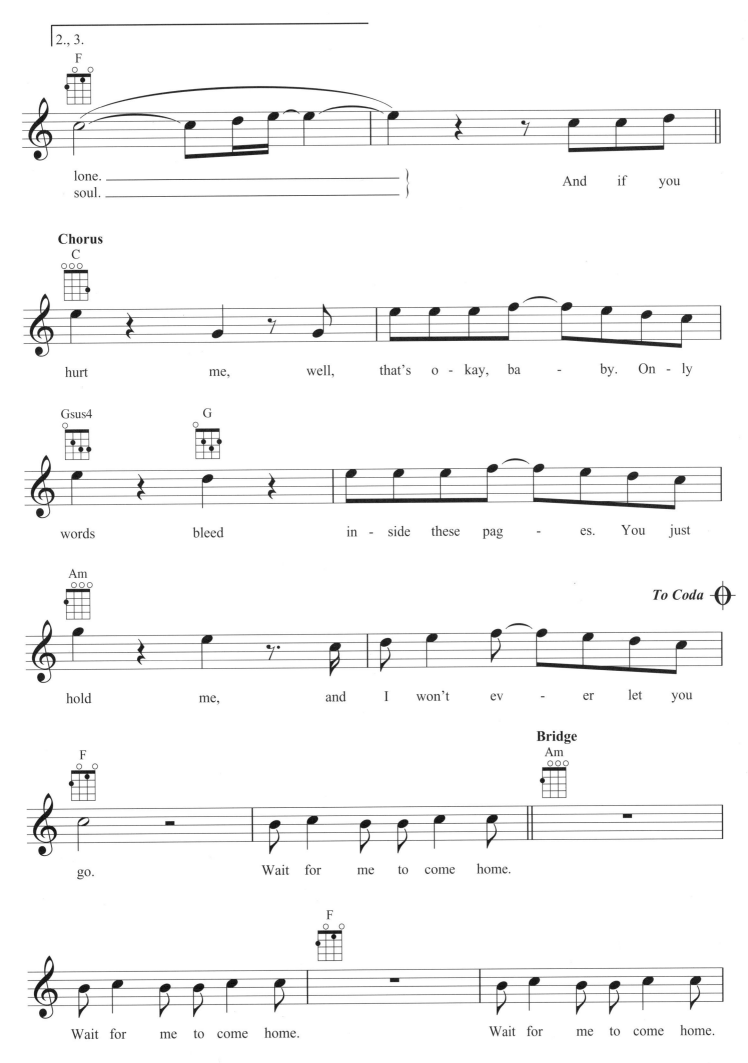

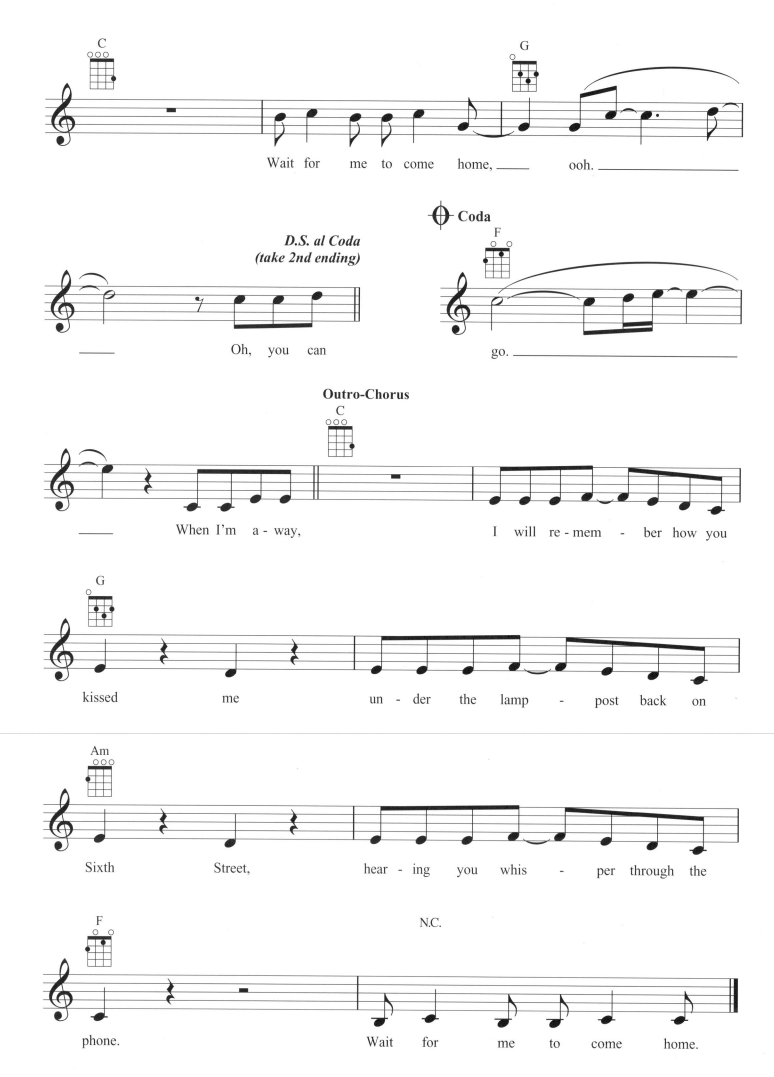

Wait for me to come home, _____ ooh. _____

D.S. al Coda
(take 2nd ending)

_____ Oh, you can

⊕ **Coda**

go. _____

Outro-Chorus

_____ When I'm a - way, I will re - mem - ber how you

kissed me un - der the lamp - post back on

Sixth Street, hear - ing you whis - per through the

phone. Wait for me to come home.

Lego House

Words and Music by Ed Sheeran, Chris Leonard and Jake Gosling

done,   I think I love you bet - ter now.   I'm out of sight,

I'm out of mind.   I'll do it all   for you in time. ____

____   And out of   all these things I've   done,   I think I

To Coda 1 ⊕
To Coda 2 ⊕

love   you   bet - ter now.   Now. ____

Verse

2. I'm gon - na

paint you by num - bers   and col - our you ____ in.

If things go right, we can frame it and

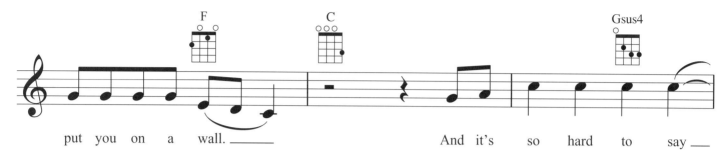

put you on a wall. _____ And it's so hard to say _____

_____ it, but I've been here be-fore. _____

_____ Now I'll sur-ren-der up _____ my

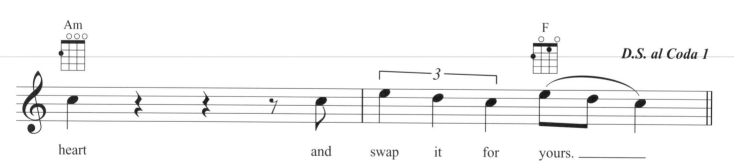

D.S. al Coda 1

heart and swap it for yours. _____

Coda 1

Bridge

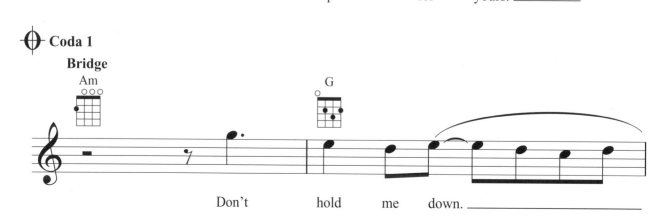

Don't hold me down. _____

x

I think the brac - es are break - ing,

and it's more than I _____ can take. _____

Coda 2
Outro-Chorus

D.S.S. al Coda 2

I'm out of touch,

I'm out of love.   I'll pick you up

when you're get - ting down.   And out of all these things I've

done,   I will love you bet - ter now.

Sing

Words and Music by Ed Sheeran and Pharrell Williams

- gram.   I want you to ___ be mine, ___ la - dy, ___ and to   hold your bod - y   close. ___

___   Take an - oth - er step   in - to the no ___ man's land   for the long - est   time, ___

𝄋 Chorus

___ la - dy. ___ I   need you, dar - ling. Come on,   set   the tone. ___ If you

feel you're fall - ing, won't you   let   me know? ___ Oh, oh, ___   ooh. ___

Oh,   oh, ___   ooh. ___

If   you love ___ me, come on,   get   in - volved. ___ Feel it   rush - ing through ___ you from your

head to toe. — Oh, oh, ————— ooh. — Oh, oh, —————

Interlude

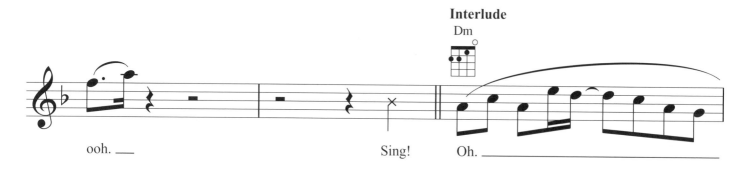

ooh. —— Sing! Oh. —————————————

————————————— Oh. ——————————————— Loud - er!

Oh. ——————————————————————————— Sing!

To Coda ⊕

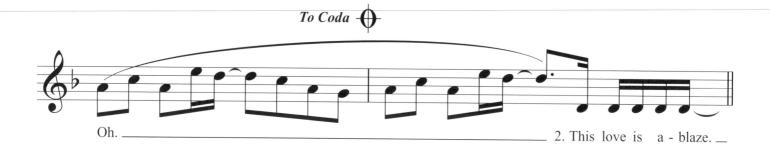

Oh. ——————————————————— 2. This love is a - blaze. —

Verse

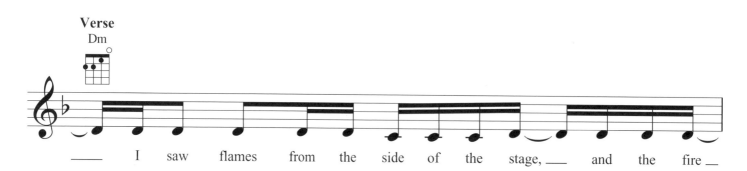

—— I saw flames from the side of the stage, — and the fire —

bri - gade comes in a cou - ple of days. ___ Un - til

then, we got noth - in' to say ___ and noth - in' to know but

some - thin' to drink ___ and may - be some - thin' to smoke.

Gm

Let it go un - til our roads are changed, _ sing - ing we found love in a lo - cal rave. _ No,

I don't real - ly know what I'm sup - posed to say, ___ but I can

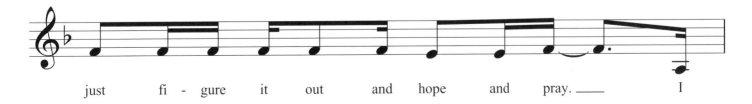

just fi - gure it out and hope and pray. ___ I

told her my name __ and said, "It's nice to meet __ ya." Then she

hand - ed me a bot - tle of wa - ter with te - qui - la.

I al - read - y know it, she's a keep - er, just from this one small act of kind - ness. I'm in

deep _____ if an - y - bod - y finds out I'm meant __

_____ to drive home. But I've drunk all of it; now I'm not.

So - ber - ing up, we just sit on the couch. __ One thing __

_____ led to an - oth - er. Now she's kiss - ing my mouth. _ I

Coda

Bridge

Can you feel _____ it? All the guys in here don't

e - ven wan - na dance. _ Can you feel _____ it? All that I can hear is

mu - sic from the back. _ Can you feel _____ it? Found you hid - ing here, so

won't you take my hand, _____ dar - ling, be - fore the beat kicks in a -

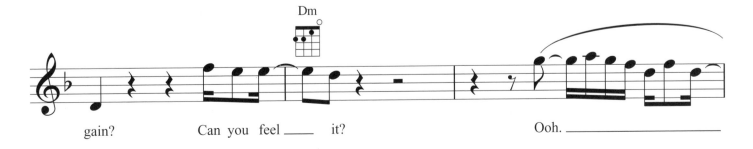

gain? Can you feel ___ it? Ooh. _____

Can you feel _____ it? _____

Oh, ___ no, ___ no, _____ no. _____

Outro-Chorus

Sing! I need you, dar - ling. Come on,
If you love ___ me, come on,

set the tone. ___ If you feel you're fall - ing, won't you
get in - volved. ___ Feel it rush - ing through ___ you from your

let me know? _ } Oh, oh, _____ ooh. ___   Oh, oh, ___
head to toe. ___ }

ooh. ___

Sing!

Sing!

One

Words and Music by Ed Sheeran

hopes   and   dreams __   and   just   stay _____   with   me? __

Chorus

_____   Ooh. _____   All   my   sens - es

come   to   life __   while   I'm   stum - bling   home   as

drunk   as   I ___   have   ev - er   been.   And   I'll   nev -

- er   leave __   a - gain, _____   'cause

you are the on - ly one. __ And all my friends have

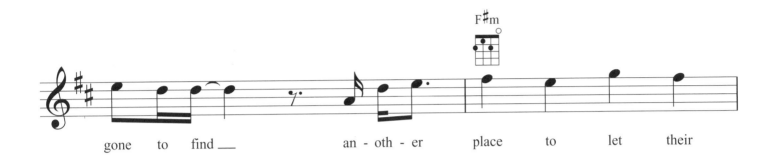

gone to find __ an - oth - er place to let their

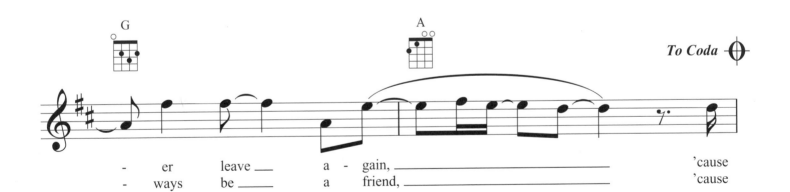

hearts col - lide. __ Just prom - ise me __ { (1.) you'll nev -
{ (2., 3.) you'll al -

To Coda ⊕

- er leave __ a - gain, _____ 'cause
- ways be __ a friend, _____ 'cause

1.

you are the on - ly one.
you are the on - ly one.

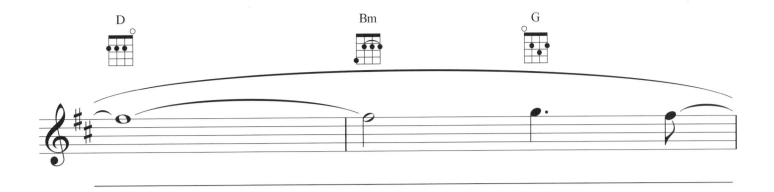

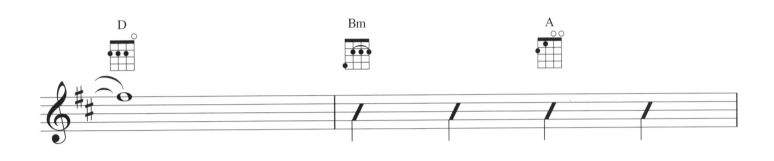

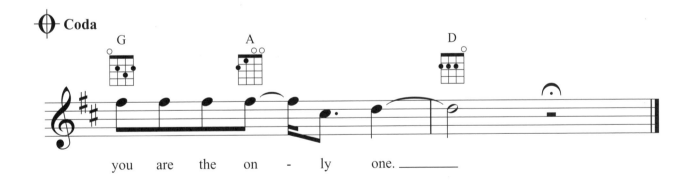

you are the on - ly one. _____

Additional Lyrics

2. Take my hand and my heart and soul.
   I will only have these eyes for you.
   And you know, everything changes,
   But we'll be strangers if we see this through.

Pre-Chorus: You could stay within these walls and bleed,
   Or just stay with me, oh, Lord, now.

Small Bump

Words and Music by Ed Sheeran

and hold _____ me __ tight. __

You are my one ___ and on - ly. ___

You can wrap your fin - gers 'round __ my thumb __ and hold __

_____ me __ tight, ___ and you'll __ be al - right. __

1.

2.

Bridge

Ooh, you're just __ a

Then you can lie with me, __ with your ti -

ny feet. When you're half a - sleep, I'll leave you __ be,

right in front of me ___ for a cou-ple weeks, so, I

can keep you ___ safe. _____

D.S. al Coda

'Cause you are my one ___

Coda

'Cause you were just a small ___

Outro

___ bump, un - born for four ___ months, then torn from life. ___

___ May-be you were need - ed up there, but we're ___

___ still ___ un - a - ware as why.

Thinking Out Loud

Words and Music by Ed Sheeran and Amy Wadge

will ___ be lov-ing you   till ___ we're sev-en-ty. _____
soul ___ could nev-er grow   old; ___ it's ev-er-green. _____

___   And, ba-by, my
___   And, ba-by, your

heart ___ could still feel as   hard ___ at twen-ty-three. _____
smile's _ for-ev-er in   my mind ___ and mem-o-ry. _____

_____   And I'm think-ing 'bout   how _____
_____   And I'm think-ing 'bout   how _____

Pre-Chorus

peo-ple fall in love in mys-te - ri-ous ways, _____
peo-ple fall in love in mys-te - ri-ous ways, _____   and

may-be just the touch of a hand. _____   Well,
may-be it's all part of a plan. _____   Well,

me, I fall in love with you ev - 'ry sin - gle day, _____ and
I'll just keep on mak - ing the same _____ mis - takes, _____

I just wan - na tell you I am. _____ So, hon - ey, now, _____
hop - ing that you'll un - der - stand _____ that, ba - by, now... _____

Chorus

_____ } take me in - to your lov - ing arms. ___

_____ Kiss me un - der the light of a

thou - sand stars. _____ Place your head on my beat - ing heart. ___

_____ I'm think - ing out _____ loud; _____ may - be

we found love right where we are. where we are. ___

Interlude

(La, la,

la, la, la, la, la, la, la, la, la, la, la.)

D.S. al Coda

Coda

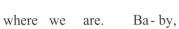

So, ba-by, now, ___ where we are. Ba-by,

Outro

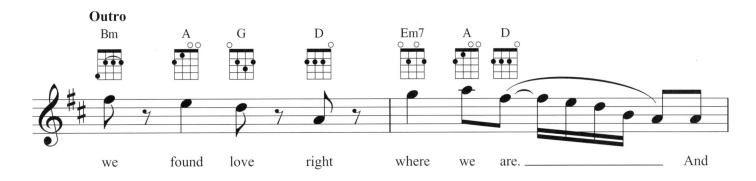

we found love right where we are. ___ And

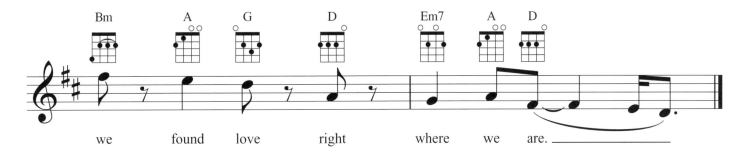

we found love right where we are. ___